HORRORS

HORRORS

Great Stories of Fear and Their Creators

Written by
ROCKY WOOD

Illustrated by
GLENN CHADBOURNE

McFarland & Company, Inc., Publishers
Jefferson, North Carolina, and London

LIBRARY OF CONGRESS CATALOGUING-IN-PUBLICATION DATA

Wood, Rocky.
Horrors : great stories of fear and their creators /
written by Rocky Wood ; illustrated by Glenn Chadbourne.
p.   cm.

ISBN 978-0-7864-4563-9
softcover : 50# alkaline paper ∞

1. Horror tales—History and criticism—Comic books, strips, etc.
2. Horror tales—Authorship—Comic books, strips, etc.
3. Graphic novels.   I. Chadbourne, Glenn, 1959–   II. Title.
PN3435.W67   2010   809.3'8738—dc22   2010031714

British Library cataloguing data are available

Cover illustrated by Glenn Chadbourne

Manufactured in the United States of America

McFarland & Company, Inc., Publishers
Box 611, Jefferson, North Carolina 28640
www.mcfarlandpub.com

For Rick Hautala, who gave me my start. Friends to the end!
Glenn Chadbourne

Table of Contents

Introduction   1

Frankenstein   9

The Vampyre   69

Death of the Diodati   91

Beowulf   105

Shakespeare   117

The Rise of the Gothic Novel   123

Poe   127

Dracula   137

Conclusion   173

Afterword   183

A dark and stormy night—Europe, 1816—The Year Without a Summer. Men of science would later put the climatic aberration down to the explosion of Mount Tambora. That year, England's literary giants Byron and Shelley were neighbors in Switzerland. Impressed by mighty nature, they watched the magnificent thunderstorms which raged over Lake Geneva and the Alps:

Introduction

From peak to peak, the rattling crags among
Leaps the live thunder! Not from one lone cloud,
But every mountain now hath found a tongue,
And Jura answers, through her misty shroud,
Back to the joyous Alps, who call to her aloud!

It proved a wet and ungenial summer, incessant rain kept the poets and their guests confined indoors at Byron's Villa Diodati for days on end. The evenings would pass, with talk of science, literature, philosophy, politics and the supernatural. They were a scandalous and intellectual group:

LORD GEORGE BYRON, a famous and controversial poet who had scandalized society with his affairs with married women, carousing and debts, and amours with a string of young society ladies.

PERCY BYSSHE SHELLEY, another famous for his poetry and his radical views about both politics and religion. Another man with an eye for the ladies, he had abandoned his pregnant wife to run away with Mary.

Shelley's lover, MARY WOLLSTONECRAFT GODWIN, had run away with him two years earlier, aged only sixteen.

CLAIRE CLAREMONT was Mary's stepsister and sometime lover of Byron. He had initially rejected her presence in Switzerland but, after finding she was pregnant with his child, had resumed their affair.

And JOHN POLIDORI, who had recently entered Byron's service as his personal physician.

On this evening, 19 June, Byron recalled their joint reading of German ghost stories to pass the time. This had become tedious and he made a new proposal:

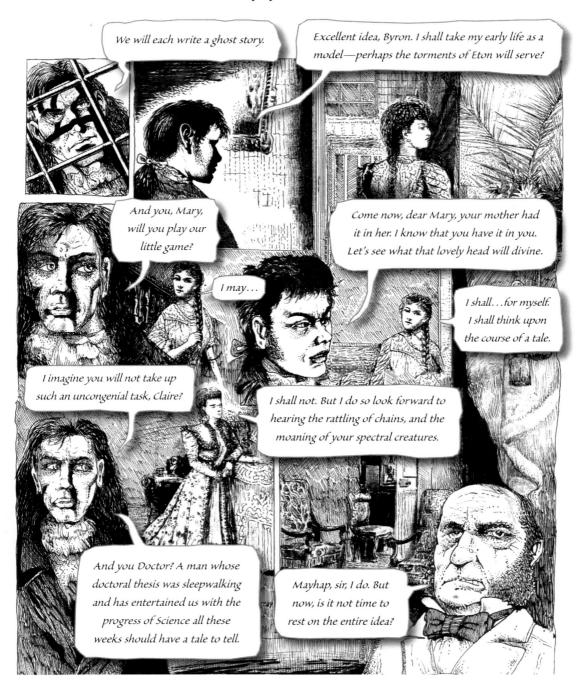

All but Claire had accepted Byron's challenge. Those few words would create Horror as we know it today. Two triumphant tales would result. But, Fate would demand a price. Tragedy lay in wait, stalking the entire group.

The party headed to bed, still conversing over the novel task...

Mary lay still, thinking of the many long conversations between the three men, discussing the principles of Life, philosophy and the strange new science of galvanism, through which even a corpse might be reanimated.

The radical talk conspired with Mary's bright imagination and influenced her dreams:

I saw the pale student of unhallowed arts kneeling beside the thing he had put together. I saw the hideous phantasm of a man stretched out, and then, on the working of some powerful engine, show signs of life, and stir with uneasy, half vital motion. Frightful it must be, for supremely frightful would be the effect of any human endeavour to mock the stupendous mechanism of the Creator of the world.

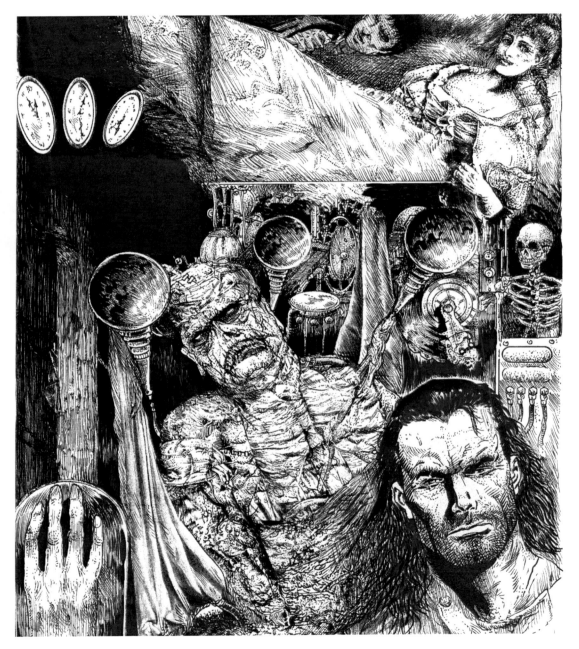

His success would terrify the artist; he would rush away from his odious handywork, horror-stricken.

5

He would hope that, left to itself, the slight spark of life he had communicated would fade; that this thing, which had received such imperfect animation, would subside into dead matter; and he might sleep in the belief that the silence of the grave would quench forever the transient existence of the hideous corpse which he had looked upon as the cradle of life.

The dream turned yet darker, a fully formed nightmare.

He sleeps; but he is awakened; he opens his eyes; behold the horrid thing stands at his bedside, opening his curtain, and looking on him with yellow, watery, but speculative eyes.

Mary awoke in terror. But, as that thrill of fear ran through her body, the story-line had formed in her mind.

She looked at the room, moonlight shining through the shutters from that great Orb in the sky, reflecting from the glassy lake and Alps beyond...

...and the hideous phantom remained.

Frankenstein

Within days Mary Godwin began her ghost story. With Percy Shelley's support it would became a novel—one of the most famous novels ever created. Indeed, creation, followed by destruction, were Mary's themes...and would presage the same pattern in her life...and that of her friends.

We begin as, Robert Walton, the captain of a ship bound for the North Pole, adventure, scientific discovery, maybe even the Northwest Passage of fable, penned a letter to his sister in England, detailing the progress of his dangerous mission...

So strange an accident has happened to us that I cannot forbear recording it, although it is very probable that you will see me before these papers can come into your possession.

Last Monday we were nearly surrounded by ice, which closed in the ship on all sides... Our situation was somewhat dangerous. Then we perceived a low carriage, fixed on a sledge and drawn by dogs, pass on towards the north, at the distance of half a mile: a being which had the shape of a man, but apparently of gigantic stature, sat in the sledge, and guided the dogs. We watched the rapid progress of the traveler with our telescopes, until he was lost among the distant inequalities of the ice.

You may conceive my astonishment the next morning when I was upon deck, and found the sailors busy on one side of the vessel. It was another sledge, like that we had seen before, which had drifted towards us in the night, on a large fragment of ice.

Only one dog remained alive; but there was a human being within it. His limbs were nearly frozen, and his body dreadfully emaciated by fatigue and suffering. I never saw a man in so wretched a condition.

We accordingly brought him back to the deck and restored him to animation by rubbing him with brandy and forcing him to swallow a small quantity. As soon as he showed signs of life we wrapped him up in blankets and placed him near the chimney of the kitchen stove. By slow degrees he recovered, and ate a little soup, which restored him wonderfully. Two days passed in this manner before he was able to relate his awful tale...

I am Victor Frankenstein, Genovese, and my family is one of the most distinguished of that Republic. For a long time I was my parents' only care, although they much desired a daughter. In their kindness they adopted a young orphan girl, Elizabeth Lavenza...she would one day be my love.

When I had attained the age of seventeen I should became a student at the University of Ingolstadt, a center of the mysterious Illuminati, who seek always to improve mankind. There, I was introduced to the wonders of natural philosophy and particularly chemistry in the laboratory of M. Waldman.

He explained to me the uses of his various machines; instructing me as to what I ought to procure, and promising me the use of his own when I should have advanced far enough in the science not to derange their mechanism.

I am happy to have gained a disciple; and if your application equals your ability, I have no doubt of your success.

He continued his lecture: 'The modern philosophers have indeed performed miracles. They've learned to penetrate into the recesses of nature; they have discovered how the blood circulates, and the nature of the air we breathe. They have acquired almost unlimited powers; they can command the thunders of heaven, and even mock the invisible world with its own shadows.'

Thus ended a day memorable to me; it decided my future destiny.

I now became consumed by the desire to uncover the secret of life. To examine the causes of life, we must first have recourse to death. I became acquainted with the science of anatomy: but this was not sufficient, I must also observe the natural decay and corruption of the human body.

After days and nights of incredible labor and fatigue, I succeeded in discovering the cause of generation and life; nay, more, I became myself capable of bestowing animation upon lifeless matter.

Armed with the knowledge he had long sought, young Victor Frankenstein feverishly fashioned a creature from purloined body parts. Hidden away in his apartment, with no-one to perceive his compulsion, he began the construction of an animate creature...

As the minuteness of the parts formed a great hindrance to my speed, I resolved to make the being of a gigantic stature; about eight feet in height, and proportionally large.

In the midst of a storm he took the last fateful step...

It was on a dreary night of November, that I beheld the accomplishment of my toils. With an anxiety that almost amounted to agony, I collected the instruments of life around me, that I might infuse a spark of being into the lifeless thing that lay at my feet. It was already one in the morning; the rain pattered dismally against the panes, and my candle was nearly burnt out, when, by the glimmer of the half-extinguished light, I saw the dull yellow eye of the creature open; it breathed hard, and a convulsive motion agitated its limbs.

In an instant the shutters dropped from the creator's eyes as he beheld the monstrosity.

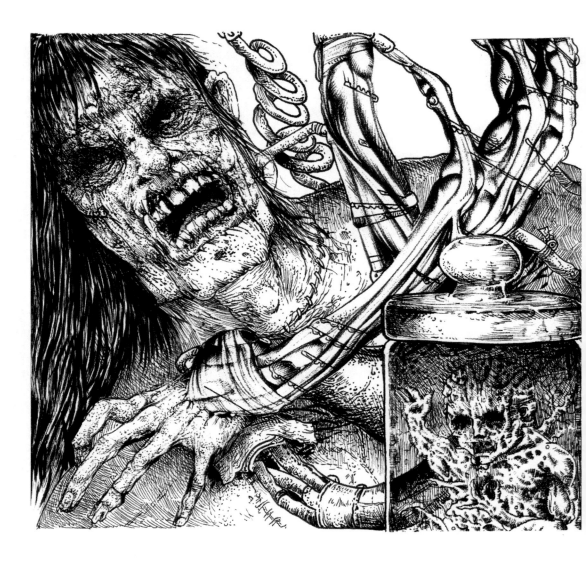

How can I describe my emotions at this catastrophe, or how delineate the wretch whom with such infinite pains and care I had endeavoured to form? His limbs were in proportion, and I had selected his features as beautiful. Beautiful! Great God! His yellow skin scarcely covered the work of muscles and arteries beneath; his hair was of a lustrous black, and flowing; his teeth of a pearly whiteness; but these luxuriances only formed a more horrid contrast with his watery eyes, that seemed almost of the same color as the dun white sockets in which they were set, his shriveled complexion and straight black lips.

But now that I had finished, the beauty of the dream vanished, and breathless horror and disgust filled my heart.

Stunned and confused Victor fled to his bedchamber, perforce to sleep. But...

When I thought of him, I gnashed my teeth, my eyes became inflamed, and I ardently wished to extinguish that life which I had so thoughtlessly made.

At length lassitude succeeded to the tumult I had before endured; and I threw myself on the bed in my clothes, endeavouring to seek a few moments of forgetfulness. But it was in vain. I slept, indeed, but I was disturbed by the wildest dreams. I thought I saw Elizabeth, my love, in the bloom of health, walking in the streets of Ingolstadt.

Delighted and surprised, I embraced her; but as I imprinted the first kiss on her lips, they became livid with the hue of death; her features appeared to change, and I thought that I held the corpse of my dead mother in my arms; a shroud enveloped her form, and I saw the grave-worms crawling in the folds of the flannel.

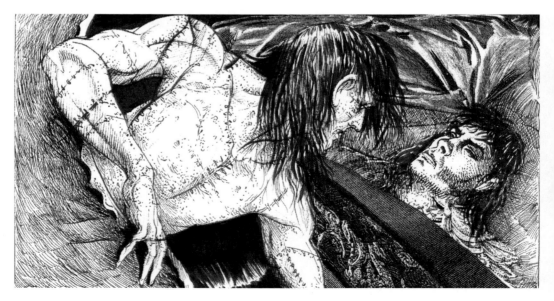

I started from my sleep with horror; a cold dew covered my forehead: when, by the dim and yellow light of the moon, as it forced its way through the window shutters, I beheld the wretch. His jaws opened, and he muttered some inarticulate sounds, while a grin wrinkled his cheeks.

One hand was stretched out, seemingly to detain me, but I escaped, and rushed down stairs. I took refuge in the courtyard; where I remained during the rest of the night, walking up and down in the greatest agitation, fearing each sound as if it were to announce the approach of the demoniacal corpse to which I had so miserably given life.

Shunned by his creator, confused, the creature also escaped the apartment, and Ingolstadt.

Forsaken monster that I was, I found my way to the
woods and took shelter in a hovel, where I passed the
winter watching and learning the ways of humanity
from a family in the next cottage.

I listened and learned that young Felix and Agatha looked after an old man as they lived their simple ways. The old man was blind and I resolved to speak to him when, alone, his lack of sight would not signal my horrid visage.

The name of the old man was *De Lacey* and the day presented itself when he was quite alone, so I came out from my hiding place.

I am an unfortunate and deserted creature, I look around and I have no relation or friend upon earth.

Do not despair. The hearts of men, when unprejudiced by any obvious self-interest, are full of brotherly love and charity.

At that instant the cottage door was opened, and Felix and Agatha entered. Who can describe their horror and consternation on beholding me? Agatha fainted. Felix darted forward, and with supernatural force tore me from his father, to whose knees I clung, in a transport of fury, he dashed me to the ground and struck me violently with a stick.

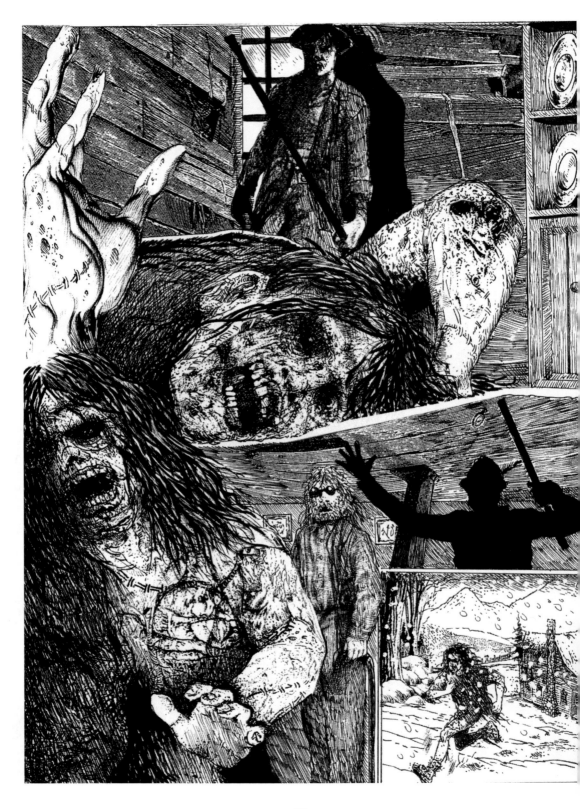

I could have torn him limb from limb, as the lion rends the antelope. But my heart sank within me as with bitter sickness, and I refrained. I saw him on the point of repeating his blow, when, overcome by pain and anguish, I quitted the cottage and escaped.

From that moment I declared everlasting war against the species, and more than all, against him who had formed me and sent me forth to this insupportable misery.

In Ingolstadt, Victor returned to more normal studies, hoping the specter of his unnatural creation is forever gone from his life. But fate is not finished with our scientist, as he receives a letter from his father.

Your lovely young brother William is dead!—that sweet child, whose smiles delighted and warmed my heart, who was so gentle, yet so gay! Victor, he is murdered!

Grief-stricken, Victor hurried to Geneva. He arrived at night; the gates of Geneva shut. He determined to find the place in the woods his father had written that the lost boy's body had lain.

I perceived in the gloom a figure—a flash of lightning illuminated the object, its gigantic stature, the deformity of its aspect. Nothing in human shape could have destroyed my fair brother. He, the filthy daemon to whom I had given life, was the murderer!

36

Next morning, at the Frankenstein home, Victor discovers that Justine Moritz, a kind, gentle girl who had been adopted by the Frankenstein household, had been accused of poor William's murder! Yet, *he* perceived the truth—the monster, not the girl, was responsible.

Justine Moritz! Poor, poor girl, is she the accused? But it is
wrongfully; every one knows that; no one believes it, surely?

But I cannot reveal the truth. My tale is not one to announce publicly;
its astounding horror would be looked upon as madness by the vulgar.

By my omission Justine was convicted and condemned to die by the throwing of black ballots.

The poor victim felt not as I did, such deep and bitter agony. She was sustained by innocence, but the fangs of remorse tore my bosom and would not forego their hold. The monster had another victim—another burden to my eternal soul.

More despondent than ever Victor decided to climb nearby Montanvert, hoping nature would revive his spirits.

But the monster had sought a similar retreat.

Devil, do you dare approach me? And do not you fear the fierce vengeance of my arm wreaked on your miserable head? That I could, with the extinction of your miserable existence, restore those victims whom you have so diabolically murdered!

Listen to my tale, when you have heard that, abandon or commiserate me, as you shall judge that I deserve. Remember, that I am thy creature: I ought to be thy Adam; but I am rather the fallen angel. Come to my ice-cave and listen to my woeful tale.

I felt what the duties of a creator towards his creature were, and that I ought to render him happy before I complained of his wickedness.

In relating his tale—shunned by all, including the old blind man's family, the monster came to admit the murder of William.

The child still struggled and loaded me with epithets which carried despair to my
heart; I grasped his throat to silence him, and in a moment he lay dead at my feet.

44

Unfeeling, heartless creator! You had endowed me with perceptions and passions, and then cast me abroad an object for the scorn and horror of mankind.

By this I was moved. I shuddered when I thought of the possible consequences of my consent, but there was some justice in his argument. The feelings he now expressed proved him to be a creature of fine sensations, and did I not, as his maker, owe him all the portion of happiness that it was in my power to bestow? I agreed, upon the condition that both creatures abandon Europe for the desolation of the South American jungles.

I determined to visit some remote spot of Scotland and finish my work in solitude. I did not doubt but that the monster followed me and would discover himself to me when I should have finished, that he might receive his companion. With this resolution I traversed the northern highlands and fixed on one of the remotest of the Orkneys as the scene of my labors. It was a place fitted for such a work, being hardly more than a rock whose high sides were continually beaten upon by the waves.

I worked on, and my labor was already considerably advanced. As I sat, a train of reflection occurred to me which led me to consider the effects of what I was now doing. Now, for the first time, the wickedness of my promise burst upon me; I shuddered to think that future ages might curse me as their pest, whose selfishness had not hesitated to buy its own peace at the price, perhaps, of the existence of the whole human race.

I trembled and my heart failed within me, when, on looking up, I saw by the light of the moon the daemon at the casement. A ghastly grin wrinkled his lips as he gazed on me, where I sat fulfilling the task which he had allotted to me. Yes, he had followed me in my travels; he had loitered in forests, hid himself in caves; and he now came to mark my progress and claim the fulfilment of my promise.

As I looked on him, his countenance expressed the utmost extent of malice and treachery. I thought with a sensation of madness on my promise of creating another like to him, and trembling with passion, tore to pieces the thing on which I was engaged. I almost felt as if I had mangled the living flesh of a human being.

The wretch saw me destroy the creature on whose future existence he depended for happiness, and with a howl of devilish despair and revenge, withdrew.

Vowing to put the past away and to build a new life, Victor now determined to marry Elizabeth. This man who so tempts the Fates!

I fear, my beloved girl, little happiness remains for us on earth; yet all that I may one day enjoy is centered in you. Chase away your idle fears; to you alone do I consecrate my life and my endeavors for contentment. I have one secret, Elizabeth, a dreadful one; when revealed to you, it will chill your frame with horror, and then, far from being surprised at my misery, you will only wonder that I survive what I have endured.

I will confide this tale of misery and terror to you the day after our marriage shall take place, for there must be perfect confidence between us. But until then, I conjure you, do not mention or allude to it. This I most earnestly entreat, and I know you will comply.

For you Victor, my true love, I shall agree glad of heart.

After the wedding ceremony was performed a large party assembled at my father's, but it was agreed that Elizabeth and I should commence our journey by water, sleeping that night at Evian and continuing our voyage on the following day. The day was fair, the wind favourable; all smiled on our nuptial embarkation. On arrival in Evian we then retired to an inn.

Elizabeth retired and I walked up and down the passages and inspecting every corner that might afford a retreat to my adversary, but I discovered no trace of him, when suddenly I heard a shrill and dreadful scream.

It came from the room into which Elizabeth had retired. As I heard it, the whole truth rushed into my mind, my arms dropped, the motion of every muscle and fiber was suspended.

This state lasted but for an instant; the scream was repeated, and I rushed into the room. Great God! Why did I not then expire! Why am I here to relate the destruction of the best hope and the purest creature on earth?

She was there, lifeless, thrown across the bed, her hair hanging down, and her pale and distorted features half covered by her hair.

I felt a kind of panic on seeing the pale yellow light of the moon. The shutters had been thrown back; and with horror I saw at the open window a most hideous figure— a grin was on the face of the monster as with his fiendish finger he pointed towards the corpse of my wife.

The horror was too large and I slumped, lacking all conscious thought, to the floor. When I awoke, Elizabeth had been moved from the posture in which I had first beheld her, and now, I might have supposed her asleep. I rushed towards her and embraced her with ardor, but the deadly languor and coldness of the limbs told me that what I now held in my arms had ceased to be the Elizabeth whom I had loved and cherished. The murderous mark of the fiend's grasp was on her neck.

I rushed towards the window, and drawing a pistol from my bosom, fired; but he eluded me, leaped from his station, and running with the swiftness of lightning, plunged into the lake.

Victor Frankenstein had no choice now but to address the heavy toll of hubris.

By the sacred earth on which I kneel, by the shades that wander near me, by the deep and eternal grief that I feel, I swear; and by thee, O Night, and the spirits that preside over thee, to pursue the daemon who caused this misery, until he or I shall perish in mortal conflict.

I was hurried away by fury; revenge alone endowed me with strength and composure; it moulded my feelings and allowed me to be calculating and calm at periods when otherwise delirium or death would have been my portion.

When I quitted Geneva my first labor was to gain some clue by which I might trace the steps of my fiendish enemy. I pursued him, and for many months this has been my task. Guided by a slight clue, I followed the windings of the Rhone, but vainly.

The blue Mediterranean appeared, and by a strange chance, I saw the fiend enter by night and hide himself in a vessel bound for the Black Sea. I took my passage in the same ship, but he escaped, I know not how.

Amidst the wilds of Tartary and Russia, although he still evaded me, I have ever followed in his track. Sometimes the peasants, scared by this horrid apparition, informed me of his path; sometimes he himself, who feared that if I lost all trace of him I should despair and die, left some mark to guide me. The snows descended on my head, and I saw the print of his huge step on the white plain.

Finally, horror-struck villagers reported a gigantic monster had taken a sledge, drawn by numerous trained dogs, and pursued his journey across the sea in a direction that led to no land; and they conjectured that he must speedily be destroyed by the breaking of the ice or frozen by the eternal frosts.

On hearing this information I suffered a temporary access of despair. I must commence a destructive and almost endless journey across the mountainous ices of the ocean, amidst cold that few of the inhabitants could long endure and which I, the native of a genial and sunny climate, could not hope to survive. I exchanged my land-sledge for one fashioned for the inequalities of the frozen ocean, and purchasing a plentiful stock of provisions, I departed.

I should guess that I had passed three weeks in this journey when suddenly my eye caught a dark speck upon the dusky plain. I strained my sight to discover what it could be and uttered a wild cry of ecstasy when I distinguished a sledge and the distorted proportions of a well-known form within.

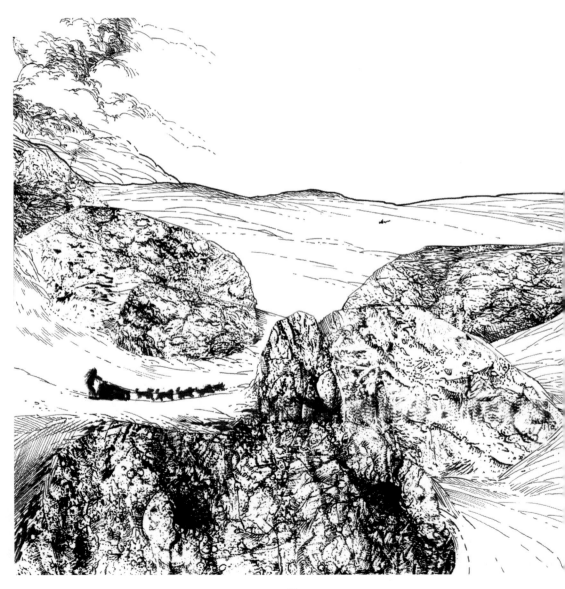

The sledge remained visible, nor did I again lose sight of it except at the moments when for a short time some ice-rock concealed it with its intervening crags. I indeed perceptibly gained on it, and when, after nearly two days' journey, I beheld my enemy at no more than a mile distant, my heart bounded within me.

But now, when I appeared almost within grasp of my foe, my hopes were suddenly extinguished, and I lost all trace of him more utterly than I had ever done before.

A ground sea was heard; the thunder of its progress, as the waters rolled and swelled beneath me, became every moment more ominous and terrific. I pressed on, but in vain. The wind arose; the sea roared; and, as with the mighty shock of an earthquake, it split and cracked with a tremendous and overwhelming sound.

The work was soon finished; in a few minutes a tumultuous sea rolled between me and my enemy, and I was left drifting on a scattered piece of ice that was continually lessening and thus preparing for me a hideous death. In this manner I myself was about to sink under the accumulation of distress when I saw your vessel, dear Walton, riding at anchor and holding forth to me hopes of succour and life.

Victor, already close to expiry when rescued, prepared to die.

The forms of the beloved dead flit before me, and I hasten to their arms. Farewell, Walton! Seek happiness in tranquility and avoid ambition, even if it be only the apparently innocent one of distinguishing yourself in science and discoveries. Learn from my miseries and not seek to increase your own.

Victor's eyes closed forever, while the irradiation of a gentle smile passed away from his lips.

63

Unlike the monster's creator, our tale is not yet done, as Captain Walton related in his last missive to his Mrs. Saville about this tawdry affair.

I entered the cabin where lay the remains of my ill-fated and admirable friend. Over him hung a form which I cannot find words to describe—gigantic in stature, yet uncouth and distorted in its proportions. As he hung over the coffin, his face was concealed by long locks of ragged hair; but one vast hand was extended, in color and apparent texture like that of a mummy. When he heard the sound of my approach, he ceased to utter exclamations of grief and horror and sprung towards the window. Never did I behold a vision so horrible as his face, of such loathsome yet appalling hideousness. I shut my eyes involuntarily and endeavoured to recollect what were my duties with regard to this destroyer. I called on him to stay.

Fear not that I shall be the instrument of future mischief. My work is nearly complete. Neither yours nor any man's death is needed to consummate the series of my being and accomplish that which must be done, but it requires my own.

Now that my creator finally lies lifeless I shall collect my funeral pile and consume to ashes this miserable frame. I shall no longer feel the agonies that now consume me.

I shall die.

He had sprung from the cabin-window as he said this, upon the ice-raft which lay close to the vessel.

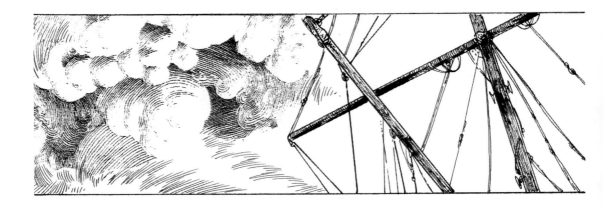

He was soon borne away by the waves, and lost in darkness and distance.

With these words Mary lay down the pen over her manuscript, which she would title *Frankenstein*, a name that had come to her in a dream.

When both Shelley and Byron's publishers rejected the story another London publisher agreed to proceed.

Frankenstein; or, the Modern Prometheus was published anonymously on 1 January 1818, and to immediate popular success.

The Vampyre

Let us now return to Dr. Polidori, also challenged by Byron that Geneva night. Soon, desperate to impress the great man, he would be found struggling for a theme, confiding to his diary: *The ghost stories begun by all but me.*

Years later Mary Shelley told of his first effort: *Poor Polidori had some terrible idea about a skull-headed lady, who was punished for peeping through a key-hole to see something very shocking and wrong; she was despatched to the tomb of the Capulets, alive.*

Byron himself had risen to the challenge. His mysterious tale was of an aristocrat, Augustus Darvell, travelling in Turkey. Strangely, he asks his companion to bury him when he dies and keep the grave's location secret. But Byron was a poet. He grew bored with the prose, and soon passed the unfinished pages around.

And one evening Byron had even read Samuel Taylor Coleridge's as yet unpublished poem *Christabel* to his guests, featuring as it does the noble female vampire, Geraldine, sucking the life force from sweet Christabel.

Suddenly Polidori was inspired—Byron's story clearly portrayed Darvell as having the characteristics of a vampire but now, for the first time, in the form of an aristocrat. And the draining of the virtuous and beautiful young girl allowed a certain sexual tension.

So Polidori began—his story would be the first published tale revealing the great secret of vampirish aristocracy. This would echo down the ages, all the way to Stephen King's Kurt Barlow and Anne Rice's Lestat. Who can separate the beautiful lie from the foul truth?

The tale begins with the unusual Lord Ruthven springing on the London scene. Pale of face, introverted and with cool grey eyes he was much sought on the social circuit; more for his singularities than his rank.

Ruthven soon caught the eye of young ladies, and of their virtuous mothers, eager to climb in society. And that of an idealistic and very eligible young gentleman named Aubrey. Orphaned young he and his beautiful sister were under the care of guardians.

Falling under the spell of Ruthven's charm, Mr. Aubrey and his guardians thought it time he take the traditional tour of Europe, joining the older man on his travels.

But once on the Continent, Ruthven became profuse in his liberality—distributing money to those who wished to wallow in lust, or gamble, or sink into iniquity.

75

This new Ruthven was a libertine—sex appeared but a lazy plaything; he gambled simply to destroy a player's fortune then deliberately lost the winnings to another, who might use the fortune to fund worse depravities.

It seemed to Aubrey all those who fell under the spell were cursed, for they all either went to the scaffold, or to the dungeon, or sunk to the lowest and most abject misery. He became sick of heart and thought to break with his companion.

The pair travelled on to Rome, where Ruthven began daily attendance upon an Italian Countess and her inexperienced daughter. There Aubrey received disturbing news from England.

An evil power must reside in Lord Ruthven, he has irresistible powers of seduction. In fine, all those females he had sought here, apparently on account of their virtue have now thrown the mask aside; and have not scrupled to expose the whole deformity of their vices to the public gaze.

Shocked by this news and Ruthven's continuing licentious behavior, Aubrey confronted his companion.

Sir, you have arranged an assignation with young Sophia this very night! This is too much! What are your intentions?

Well, sir, my intentions are such as I suppose all would have upon such an occasion.

And do you intend to marry her?

To which, his Lordship merely laughed. This final blow gave Aubrey the pretext he needed to break with Ruthven and continue his travels, fixing his new residence in the house of a Greek in Athens.

Under the same roof existed a being so beautiful and delicate that the young man fell instantly and deeply in love. The light steps of Ianthe went all across the countryside with Aubrey as he spent weeks in a trance, tracing a lost empire and revelling in her perfect beauty.

One summer's day Ianthe discoursed upon the supernatural tales told by her nurse—she shared with him the tale of the living vampire, who had passed years amongst his friends by feeding upon the life of a new and lovely female each year. Aubrey's blood ran cold, even as he attempted to laugh his beloved out of such idle and horrible fantasies.

Aubrey's laughter shocked Ianthe. She entreated her parents to warn him of the truth and both, pale with horror at the very name, affirmed the existence of these creatures: vampyre.

I warn you, never pass late through the northern wood. No Greek would ever remain there after the day closes. It is truly the resort of vampyres in their nocturnal orgies.

When Aubrey again laughed, the shock upon the faces of his audience at this mocking of the superior, infernal power, caused him to silence.

Yet, the next day Aubrey dallied too long in his wanderings and by the time he turned for home it was late. He had advanced too far, the short twilight was upon him, and a powerful storm was above. His horse bolted the lightning flashes as he rode the dreaded wood before dismounting to seek cover at a hovel that hardly lifted itself from the masses of dead leaves and brushwood.

As he did he heard the dreadful shrieks of a woman...mingling with the stifled, exultant mockery of a laugh.

Bursting into the darkened hovel he heard a voice before he was thrown with supernatural force. The life was being choked from his body by powerful hands, just as men bearing torches approached from the stormy forest. The attacker fled!

When the villagers arrived the light of the torches revealed at the base of a nearby tree a true horror—it was Ianthe! A lifeless corpse! No color was upon her cheek, nor her lip; but about her face a stillness almost as attaching as in the life that once dwelt there; upon her neck and breast was blood, and upon her throat were the marks of teeth having opened the veins. The men were struck with horror as Aubrey's mind took refuge in vacancy.

Days later Aubrey awakened from his coma,
to the visage of the very creature his fevered mind
had determined to be Ianthe's killer—Ruthven!

Panicked though he was he was instantly soothed by the nobleman's charms, almost in the form of hypnotism. Now his lordship seemed quite changed and Aubrey discounted his fevered conclusions. Within weeks the two were companions again, and seeking to repair Aubrey's broken spirit, they again travelled the provinces. And it was there they were set upon by brigands. Ruthven, mortally wounded, broached his final request:

Weary of a country where he had met with such terrible misfortunes Aubrey returned to England and the caresses of his sister, not yet eighteen, but ready to be presented to the world at the next drawing-room.

The crowd was excessive and standing in a corner Aubrey found his arm grabbed.

He could not believe it possible—the dead rise again! Ruthven moved into the crowd and was lost to sight. But soon, at a gaggle of young rakes attending to his sister, there stood Ruthven, with the young maiden raptly gazing into his eyes. His remembered oath now startled poor Aubrey—was he then to allow this monster to roam, bearing ruin upon his breath, amidst all he held dear, and not avert its progress?

Should he break his sacred oath? But who would believe him? Should he use his own hand to free the world of the wretch? But death, he remembered, had already been mocked.

And now, his mind broke once more.

Time elapsed and when, upon the last day of the year since Ruthven's first death in Greece, Aubrey came yet again out of coma. But to this news—his sister was the next day to marry the Earl of Marsden.

He called for her and she proudly displayed him a locket portrait of her love. To Aubrey's horror it showed the very features of the monster that had so long influenced his life, now disguised with another title. He bade her swear not to wed but could not break his oath to explain the circumstance.

The physicians restrained and drugged him, for his insanity had clearly returned.

Waking the next morning in instant terror Aubrey wrote a letter to his guardians laying down the whole tale of his lordship, and his misdeeds, to be read when the oath expired that very midnight. Leaving the pages by his bed he removed himself to the place where all were assembled for the nuptials.

Lord Ruthven was the first to perceive him. Speechless with rage he forced Aubrey to the staircase and spoke most directly in his ear:

Remember your oath, and know, if not my bride today, your sister is dishonored. Women are frail!

Aubrey could no longer support himself—his own rage not finding vent had broken a blood-vessel and he was conveyed to bed. That night, the marriage solemnized and the couple having left London, Aubrey expired. Shortly after Aubrey's passing the physician delivered the last letter to the guardians.

Upon reading its wholly shocking contents, they hastened to protect the former Miss Aubrey; but when they arrived it was too late. Lord Ruthven had disappeared, and Aubrey's sister had glutted the thirst of a *VAMPYRE!*

Polidori did not complete his distressing tale, simply titled *The Vampyre*, until long after his return to England. Published in *New Monthly Magazine* in 1819, along with a 'Letter to the Editor from Geneva,' which told of the Ghost story competition, it falsely implied the story was written by Byron. For this reason it was an overnight sensation and best-seller, but Polidori was quick to deny Byron's authorship:

I beg leave to state that your correspondent has been mistaken in attributing that tale, in its present form, to Lord Byron. The fact is, that though the groundwork is certainly Byron's, its development is mine, being drawn from the materials which he had said he intended to have employed in the formation of his Ghost story.

Whoever did pen the tale, the fundamentals of the true vampire were now revealed for all—the noble background; the creature that doesn't simply possess a body, but is undead and undying; the possessor of nearly irresistible seductive charms; and the compulsion to wanderlust, wreaking destruction across a wide path.

Of course, all those who had been at Villa Diodati that summer, and many who had not, recognised the lead characters in this morality tale. Byron as Lord Ruthven, the very name of the character used to disguise the real identity of the poet in Lady Caroline Lamb's novel, *Glenarvon*. Mr. Aubrey, the companion whose entire life is destroyed by the monster's charms and evils—none other than Dr. John Polidori himself.

Life will imitate fiction as the wheel of death and destiny turns yet faster.

Death of the Diodati

The summer was over and with its passing the Shelleys and Claire returned to England. No deed, good or bad, goes unpunished.

The first to pay the penalty was Fanny Imlay, half-sister of both Mary and Claire. She was in love with Percy and upset that both her siblings had run off to the Continent with him, leaving her pining and alone. In October 1816, shortly after they returned she fled to an inn in Swansea, Wales...

...where she wrote letters to Mary and her father and took an overdose of laudanum.

Percy's first wife Harriet had never recovered from the poet's abandonment of her and their two children. On 10 December 1816 she threw herself into the Serpentine in London's Hyde Park and drowned.

The suicide note read:

Before long the Diodati curse came closer to those in the Villa that night. By September of 1818 the Shelleys were back in Italy. Their one-year old daughter Clara began to suffer in the terrible summer heat—first from dysentery and then convulsions. Her parents rushed her to Venice to see Byron's preferred doctor. But before the man could be found...

The child died in her mother's arms. That night Mary wrote, *This is the Journal of misfortunes.*

In June of 1819, not a year after little Clara's death, the bright young boy fell ill and died of malaria, spread from the Tiber marshes near Rome.

William is dead! That sweet child, whose smiles delighted and warmed my heart. I shall never recover from that blow. Everything on earth has lost its interest to me.

For Mary and Percy worse was to come. They adored their son William, but he too, would be taken by the climate and ills of the Italian peninsula Percy loved so much and would not leave—even at further risk to his family.

And so the burdens of Victor Frankenstein and Lord Ruthven began to pile at the door of the Shelleys. But, what of the others—were they to be spared?

Our good doctor, Polidori had not done well since the publication of *The Vampyre*.

Unable to secure employment, hounded by claims that the tale was actually Byron's and weighed down by his gambling debts, he drank poison and died in London on 23 August 1821, just two years after the tale of Ruthven's depredations was published.

And what of Byron, Polidori's nemesis and the model for Ruthven? The child Claire was carrying that lost summer, Allegra, had been cruelly taken from her mother by the uncaring poet. He banished the young girl to the convent of San Giovanni Battista and refused to see her, or let her mother visit. Allegra fell ill with typhus at the convent in April 1822. Her three doctors *bled* her, much in the way a vampire might. Mortally weakened, she died aged only five.

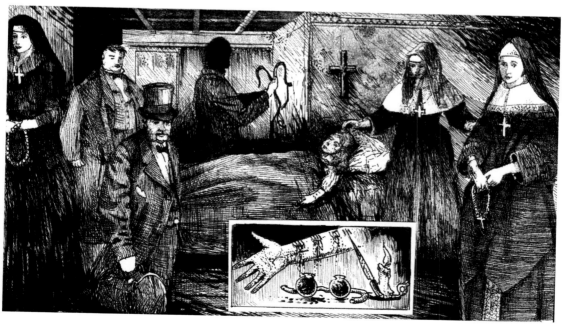

Dear Shelley—
The blow was stunning and unexpected but I have borne
up against as I best can. I suppose that Time will do
his usual work—Death has done his.

The Shelleys were still ensconced in Italy but disillusionment had set in for the young Percy, whose writings were becoming more and more melancholy. On 8 July 1822 he argued with Mary before setting out in a boat from Livorno—directly into an approaching storm. The boat was never seen again, but days later two bodies were washed ashore.

The Shelleys' friend Edward Trelawney soon identified Percy and arranged for the badly decomposed corpse to be cremated on the beach. Byron asked for Shelley's skull but was disappointed when the entire body was consumed by fire.

Byron told all who would listen the world had lost a great man.

All Mary retained of her husband was his badly charred heart, which she kept in her writing desk.

Had Byron not noted the constant approach of Death? The man's ego was of such proportion to exclude such weakness. Now the great poet threw himself into a new cause–the fight for Greek independence from the Ottoman Empire. He invested his own funds in re-fitting the Greek fleet and accepted appointment as a military commander.

Now the Fates caught up with the man described as *mad, bad and dangerous to know*. In Messolonghi he suffered a fever and the man who inspired the aristocratic vampire lord was *bled* by his doctors, which led to sepsis. On the evening of 18 April 1824 a great thunderstorm swept the area convincing his Greek friends a great soul was departing this earth. Byron died the next day.

99

The Fates' clock now ticked slow—a desperately sad Mary Wollstonecraft Shelley suffered from headaches, depression, nerves and in her later years, a mysterious paralysis. Her doctor finally diagnosed a brain tumor—perhaps the sickness of her invention infected her very thoughts—she died in London on February 1, 1851.

Her son opened Mary's box-desk. Inside he found locks of her dead children's hair, a notebook she had shared with Percy, and a page of his poetry folded around a silk parcel containing some of his ashes...and the charred remains of his heart.

Now only Claire Clairmont remained—the only one of the five from that night in June of 1816 who chose not to write a story—the only one not to die tragically. Coincidence? Fate? Who can say? Byron's lover, mother of their lost daughter, she would live to the age of 81, dying peacefully in Florence, Italy.

CLAIRE CLAREMONT
1798–1879

SHE PASSED HER LIFE
IN SUFFERINGS,
EXPIATING NOT ONLY HER FAULTS
BUT ALSO HER VIRTUES

The Creators were now Dead, but the Monsters...the Monsters still *Live*!

So, do you wonder who tells this tale? Yes? Why? It is the tale that matters, not the teller. Do you not think? For now, let us tell the tales, the horrors heard around the cave campfire, outside the gates of Megiddo, in camps surrounding Troy, in the dark forests of Europe.

The tales first taken down on Mesopotamian clay tablets, on scrolls in Egypt, with quill on parchment in Gaul...in Hispania...and Anglia. The very next books printed after the first—the Bible. Ah, the Bible, that wondrous collection of great stories—horrors visited by man upon man, greater even than those visited by God. A book of horrors indeed, as yet unsurpassed in the annals of literature.

On now to those other Tales, some you may have heard. Such as *Beowulf*, the greatest poem of the Angles and the Saxons...a story of the lands we now call Scandinavia. A tale of heroes...and a monster. Oh yes, a monster.

Beowulf

In the Dark Ages in the land we now call Denmark, a great but dissolute King, a King with an awful secret, built a great Hall. Heorot, he called it, and each night it sang with festivities—great quantities of food and drink were consumed, warriors bed wenches, and heroic songs were sung.

But this King had sinned—and sinners must be chastised. The singing, the joy of life had stirred a demon.

Grendel, shunned and miserable, lived in a nearby swamp. Taunted by the festivities at Heorot he could no longer endure his solitude.

Enraged, the demon attacked Heorot and slaughtered many of the fine warriors, none of whom could stand before its brute strength. Grendel, who had feasted for years on sheep and deer, now found the human breast a delicacy.

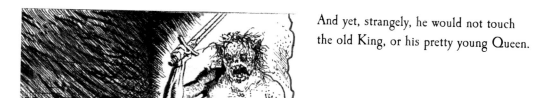

And yet, strangely, he would not touch the old King, or his pretty young Queen.

The land now needed a Hero and, from across the seas, one came. A fearless warrior of the finest Norse stock—Beowulf. Beowulf, handsome and strong, perhaps the strongest man since Hercules.

Spurning the gold King Hroogar offered him to fight and kill Grendel, Beowulf demanded only the right to Glory. That night Grendel returned, and fought Beowulf in the mightiest hand-to-hand combat ever recorded.

Beowulf finally triumphed over the monster by tearing an arm from its horrid form, before the creature, mortally wounded, fled Heorot. Grendel slunk back to the swamp to die, but not to die alone.

This would not be the end of the matter, for the King's secret was this—Grendel was his son! Hroogar had lain with the last of a race of horrid demons. Grendel's mother had appeared in the form of a lovely woman, offering Hroogar a kingdom and riches for his seed. Now, the piper must be paid—Grendel was dead. The Demon mother wreaked her revenge by slaughtering every living thing at Heorot that night, excepting the royal couple and the sleeping Beowulf.

Now, far too late, the King revealed his secret to the Hero, who set out for the lair of Grendel's mother—and a final confrontation.

Beowulf found her among the foul trophies of her son's murderous rampages.

She was the last of the entire Demon race. Beowulf drove his strong arm as he swept a great sword and struck the head from the author of Heorot's misery.

And that should be the last we hear of the mighty Beowulf—the Hero at his peak. But this is no fairy-tale...

114

In the manner of the greatest warriors, whether they are Vikings or Marines, Beowulf would die in battle—from the wounds suffered fighting a great dragon. He was old by then...and perhaps a little slow. Or perhaps his hand was momentarily stayed by the vision of a demon riding the Dragon's back?

Beowulf's tale was once *said* to be the greatest ever told.

SHAKESPEARE

Hamlet

Centuries later a great playwright emerged—so great it is said even today he is the greatest tale-teller who ever lived. *Hamlet* tells the tale of a prince's confused and tragic response to his father's regicide. The play featured what were to become William Shakespeare's horrific hallmarks: a vengeful Ghost, poisonings, real and pretended madness, unrequited love, suicide, and murder.

117

Macbeth

How now you secret, black, and midnight Hags?

Double, double, toile and trouble; Fire burne, and Cauldron bubble

Theatre folk have it this play is cursed and will not say its name—they call it *The Scottish Play*, as if misdirection could fool a Curse!

This tale of regicide, murder, ghosts and witches takes place in Scotland—a dark and gloomy land on the edge of the civilized world. Three Witches predict regicide, mass murder, hauntings and the suicide of Lady Macbeth. Macbeth's power lust finally leads to his undoing as a vengeful Macduff beheads him in battle. Witches, ghosts, blood flowing freely...mayhem, and a little justice to sate our souls.

This most famous scribe of the stage, whose works are so well-known, had dark secrets of his own. He married hastily to avoid scandal and, after the birth of his last children, Master Shakespeare simply disappears. For seven long years his whereabouts and deeds or misdeeds are unknown. Then appeared in London this fully-formed writer, perhaps the greatest of any Age. Had he been practicing his Art as a school-master? Was he abroad, learning of Tales to inspire his canon? In hiding from debtors; or a vengeful lover?

Or was he simply playing one of many Parts, in some other World?

All the world's a stage, and all the men and women merely players: they have their exits and their entrances; and one man in his time plays many parts.

The Rise of the Gothic Novel

The Castle of Otranto

Throughout history the supernatural had merged with life and so it was with humanity's tales. But, in the 18th Century, the Age of Enlightenment brought *Science* and *Reason* to the scribbler's table. Stories are never invented—in fact some argue there are only a handful of tales, told in different ways. But many scholars have opined that Horace Walpole, another Englishman, invented the Gothic Novel in 17 and 64.

At this point literature literally split between the everyday tale and those filled with the doings of other creatures, other worlds and the cruelest of all monsters—the human.

Not a quarter century passed before Matthew Lewis penned the next great Gothic novel in but ten weeks and when not yet twenty years of age. His beastly inspiration is suspected but not proven. And, in 1816, Master Lewis visited our friends Byron and the Shelleys in Geneva. What tales must have been shared!

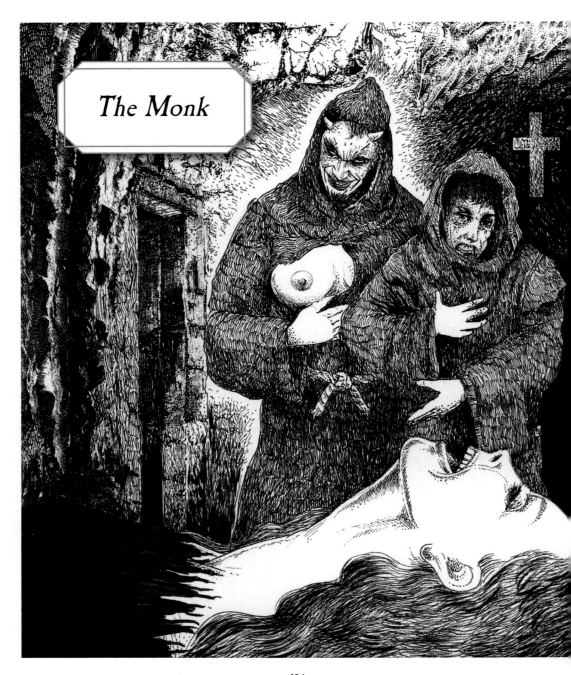

The Monk

As others expanded the gothic form, a series of characters, motifs if you will, joined our nightmares.

Let us now leave that fog-bound island off the coast of Europe for a vibrant seaport in the New World.

POE

Before Mary Shelley wrote *Frankenstein* a boy born in Boston to two actors was given the name Edgar, after a character in Shakespeare's *King Lear*. Tragedy struck young Edgar Poe early—his father ran off when he was one, the next year his mother died, and he went to live with the Allan family, becoming evermore Edgar Allan Poe.

Drifting from job to job in the publishing industry of the early 19th century, Poe became a sensation less than five years before his death, with the publication of *The Raven*.

The Raven

Tell me I implore, shall I clasp in heaven a sainted maiden whom the angels named Lenore.

Nevermore.

In one tale, a living house literally terrifies its owners to death before falling victim itself.

The Fall of the House of Usher

My brain reeled as I saw the mighty walls rushing asunder.

Now Poe gained fame but not fortune, personal tragedy swirled as his young wife soon died. And the scribbler himself was frequently drunk.

The Masque of the Red Death

And Darkness and Decay and the Red Death held illimitable dominion over all.

In another tale, indifferent nobles indulge while a great plague kills their subjects.

The Pit and the Pendulum

*I was sick unto death,
with that long agony.*

Poe also related the Terror of a victim of the Spanish Inquisition, left to die by falling into a deep pit, or being sliced in two by a swinging scythe.

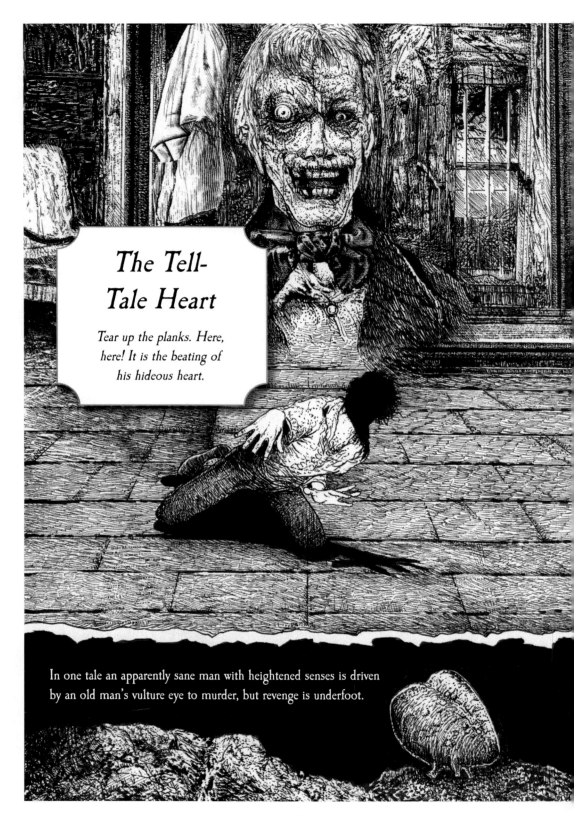

The Tell-Tale Heart

Tear up the planks. Here, here! It is the beating of his hideous heart.

In one tale an apparently sane man with heightened senses is driven by an old man's vulture eye to murder, but revenge is underfoot.

The dark-themed stories won't be repressed. A deranged man tortures and kills his cat. Murdering his wife next and hiding the body behind a wall he forgets the pet's reincarnated replacement.

In the last of Poe's great horror tales an Italian nobleman tricks his drunken enemy and traps him forever inside a wine cellar.

On October 3, 1847 Poe was found wandering the streets of Baltimore in another man's clothes, confused and in great distress.

He died a few days later, uttering the words *Lord, help my poor soul*. The cause of death was never discovered.

Dracula

Bram Stoker was an Irish born theatre manager who supplemented his income writing a series of highly sensational novels.

Irving, I shall call it The Un-Dead.

Call it what you will my dear Stoker but recall I have yet to agree to portray your Count on stage. Perhaps the Un-Dead should remain so?

THE VAMPYRE

Studying European folklore and traditions Stoker wrote a novel inspired by Dr Polidori's *The Vampyre,* and by *Carmilla,* the tale of a lesbian vampire. His brilliance was in giving the title character the aristocratic mannerisms of his dear friend and mentor, Henry Irving. It was published in 1897 and its very title inspires immortal dread: *Dracula.*

The novel begins as a young lawyer is sent to explain the purchase of a London estate to the foreign buyer. Young Jonathan Harker arrived at Castle Dracula in the province of Transylvania...

And so the English lawyer crossed the Count's threshold, soon to notice many remarkable things, including his host's hands. Strange to say, there were hairs in the centre of the palm. The nails were long and fine, and cut to a sharp point.

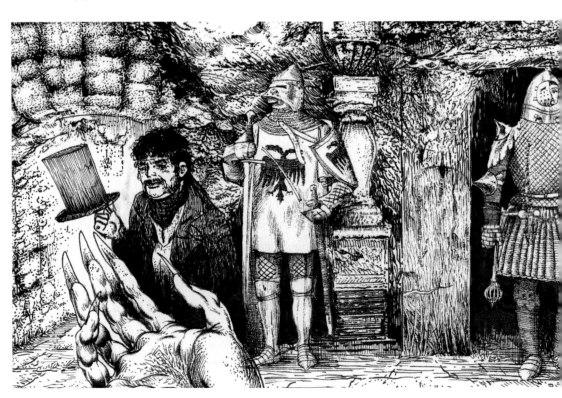

The Count took Harker on a tour of his ancient castle, which to the Victorian eye was a strange mix of Europe's now lost Middle Ages and the influences of the East, even a touch of the Turk, Jonathan thought. While fascinated, he also felt a sense of something just past strange, but shook this off as an effect of the Count's ancestry.

But Harker's visit was undertaken at great risk. The strange Count did not eat, could not be seen in a mirror, controlled wolves, and did not wish to let Mr Harker leave his decaying halls. And he warned the young man...

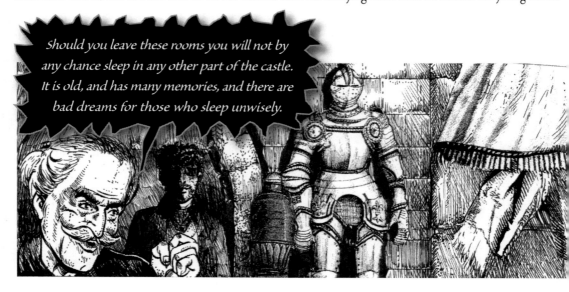

Should you leave these rooms you will not by any chance sleep in any other part of the castle. It is old, and has many memories, and there are bad dreams for those who sleep unwisely.

Harker, out of an excess of obstinacy, ignored this and chose to sleep in nearby, feminine, rooms. There he was visited by young women...each with brilliant white teeth that shone like pearls against the ruby of their voluptuous lips.

Harker fled from the scene and into the castle, quickly becoming lost.

He wandered in fear for many hours before thin light returned. Finally, he discovered the Count, lying at daylight in his dirt-filled coffin, bloated with blood. Horror redoubled.

Determined, Harker now conceived escape...and headed homeward, towards his beloved fiancée, Mina Murray.

But the Count's plans were not thwarted—the monster sailed towards the teeming blood-filled millions of England. The crew had disappeared during the transit—sustenance for the vampire.

The Count, in wolfen-form, had arrived. And at the very same town as Mina Murray and her dear friend, Lucy Westenra, the latter also recently engaged to marry.

The great vampire quickly found his lair, in a cemetery overlooking the roiling ocean. And close, so close, to the town of Whitby and the home of Miss Westenra...

And now the dance of the stalker, as the Count in his differing forms, observed his victim, slowly drawing her to his mesmeric life-force. His desire built and he began to lure Lucy...lure her, sleep-walking into the night.

The night...the virgin bride met her lover in the graveyard. A simple kiss, a bite to neck and Lucy, the vigorous young English girl, so full of life, so full of blood, was *his*...for all time.

Soon Miss Westenra was suffering the agonies of the night, dreaming, sleep-walking, the skin of her throat pierced by two little red points, like pin-pricks.

Lucy now grew ill, but of no special disease. Mina Murray attended her. Lucy looked awful and grew more ill by the day, and by the night. Desperate, Mina asked her friend Dr. John Seward to consult.

Mina, hearing from Jonathan, left for Buda Pesth, where he was recovering in a hospital. There they married. Meanwhile her friend Dr. Seward examined Lucy. Unable to discern the cause of her illness, he sent for his old friend and master, Professor Van Helsing, of Amsterdam.

Van Helsing, an expert of the strange traditions of Europe that science sought to expose as but superstition, suspected foul play, but kept his counsel. Despite his efforts Lucy could not be saved from the continuing depredations of the Count. She died and was laid to rest.

Soon after children were being attacked a beautiful young woman, each returned with throat wounds.

Babies were taken from their cribs, always at night, always returned. Always tired, exhausted even, limp and pale.

And what the victims' parents did not know...could not know, even in their fear. The young woman would always rendezvous with her Master in the town graveyard. Appraised of these new attacks Van Helsing consulted his books and formed a terrible conclusion.

He confided this analysis, this deep suspicion, to Dr Seward and his friends, Lucy's bereaved fiancé Arthur Holmwood and a dashing American, Quincey Morris. Had Lucy become a vampire? At night, they approached her erstwhile tomb, and found Lucy Westenra out among the gravestones—quite Un-Dead.

They had caught the Bride in her Act! The Lucy that was flung her latest victim to the ground, mercifull[y] unbitten; and looked to attack those would interfere with her duty, her desire. Van Helsing raised the Hol[y] Cross and horror now streaked across *her* face before she turned and fled into the night.

The intrepid group followed Arthur's lost love, now clearly a vampire bride, into her tomb, meaning to end that corruption of nature.

At Van Helsing's instruction and urging, brave Arthur struck a stake deep in the heart of the nosferatu, releasing Lucy's soul from its entrapment.

Still, a greater task was at hand—finding the Count and ending his reign of blood-soaked erotic terror. Deciphering the clues Van Helsing's team, now including the returned Jonathan and Mina Harker, realised the dreaded Count had purchased Carfax, an estate adjacent to the lunatic asylum Dr. Seward maintained below his own apartments.

A peculiar patient was held in the asylum, but regularly escaped to the great estate. Mr Renfield was tended both by his doctor and by another...flapping *his* silent way to and from Carfax. Dr Seward defined the poor unfortunate a zoophagous maniac—he constantly ate flies, spiders and birds to consume their life force. But Renfield was now also victim of the Count—who agreed to send him an endless supply of creatures in exchange for Renfield's worship.

The five Victorians—Prof. Van Helsing, Jonathan and Mina Harker, Quincey Morris and Arthur Holmwood —determined to pit their will against the ancient evil, armed with the product of both science and superstition. It was this knowledge they would exploit.

How then are we to begin our strike to destroy him? For if we fail in this our fight he must surely win, and then where end we? To fail here, is not mere life or death. It is that we become as him, that we henceforward become foul things of the night like him, without heart or conscience, preying on the bodies and the souls of those we love best.

A creature as old and wily as Count Dracula sensed the chase, and took revenge by not only biting dear Mrs Harker, but feeding her his own blood, creating a telepathic bond of control, but he was caught in the act.

166

Now revealed and under threat, the monster fled back to Transylvania, pursued by Van Helsing and his veritable posse.

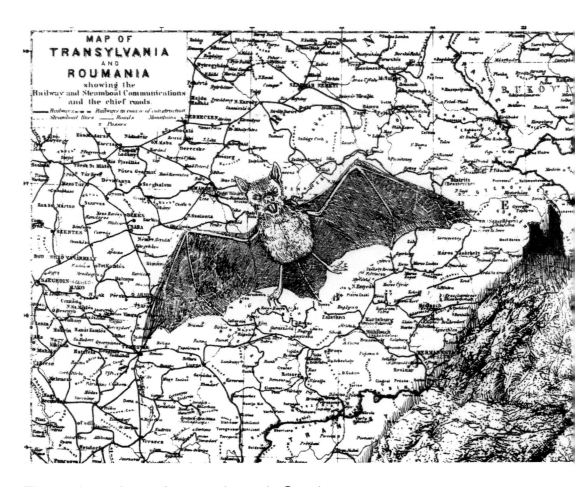

They met for one final confrontation, deep in the Carpathian mountains.

The Count, carried swiftly towards his Castle, was overtaken just short of safety. Still daylight, his only defence was a gypsy escort...the determined attackers, armed with Winchester rifles, had laid ambush.

Vicious combat followed as the gypsies sought in vain to protect their cargo but the pursuers, with their superior weapons, prevailed.

So it was that The Great Monster of the Ages, the wampyr Count known as Dracula, was outsmarted by modernists, who now came upon his bed in the fading daylight. He was despatched within sight of his great Castle, and Mina Harker was thus freed from her terrible bonds.

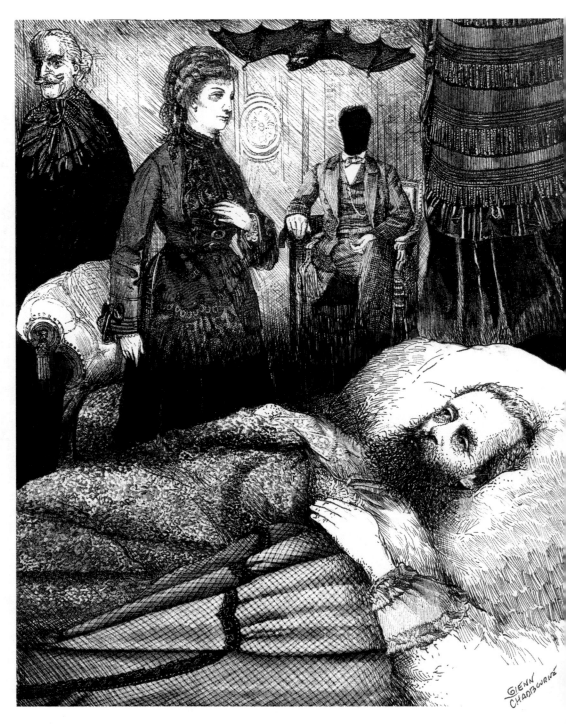

As to Mr Stoker, *Dracula* was a modest success. The author lived another 15 years, suffering from strokes. It was rumoured he died of syphilis, a disease of sexual transmission. If true, what delicious irony—for this man shocked the Victorian public with his erotic tale of sexual passion and blood transfer. And was remembered evermore.

Do you still wonder who tells this tale? Perhaps you were right before—the teller may have import. Would you like then to hear mine? Alas, my name is gone. Lost to dust, the dust of Babylon, of Egypt, of Persia, of Carthage, and of Imperial Rome's summer lanes.

Conclusion

I remember entrancing the First Man on the vast plains of Africa, and those huddling in the cold caves of Europe. I cannot remember the time before I told my first story, that of Creation. Perhaps that was the time of my birth?

I remember when I first learned to suck the tale from others...the joy it gave me...enough pleasure to last many, many years. It stole vitality from the teller but if I did not draw from them too often they could last me a lifetime—theirs, of course.

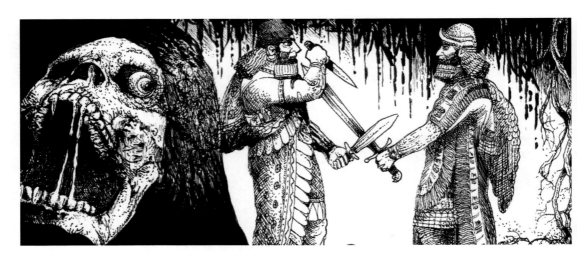

I recall the grim joy when I learnt to *influence* the tale itself. This reverse feeding—call it force-feeding, if you will—almost always destroyed the recipient. But I care not. They were but servants of story, mortal and on this earth for but a short time.

You find *my* tale hard to believe? It's the end of a wondrous four year European War that has swept away great monarchies in Germany, Austria and Hungary, and in Old Russia. A War that returns the Carpathians to their ancient isolation. A Great and Good Horror, some are even it calling *The Great War*.

But of course you should question. It is, after all, 1919, seven years since Master Stoker passed into the great beyond, an abstraction which holds no fear for me. A new World is upon us and your scientific rationality rightly questions my existence.

Shall we review the evidence then? Do you not recall the tales of pre-history, of the Time of Heroes, of the Dark Ages? The tales *I* told the troops outside the walls of Megiddo, those camped on the beaches of Troy, and the peasants in the dark forests of Germania? Who do you think *sucked* the tale of Beowulf from the forgotten poet? Who do you think watched as the events at Heorot unfolded?

By what you call the Middle Ages I had learned to *feed* the tales to my erstwhile colleagues. One was the leading Italian poet of all time. But after he passed I had to seek another.

In 1587 I found the greatest writer in the history of another language—English. A simple tutor, barely feeding wife and children, scribbling tales on scraps of purloined paper.

In the guise of wealthy benefactor I stole him away to the great libraries of Constantinople.

In 1816 I became the lowly manservant of Lord Byron, to feed both his Lordship and his neighbour Mr Shelley

Luck provided Miss Godwin and Dr Polidori, with such fresh minds, so open, so willing—two of my greatest protégés. And that I could have them tell two tales that were not just fantasy, but *truth*, stands with my greatest triumphs. The *truth* of the Vampyre tale.

When the villagers arrived the light of the torches revealed a true horror—it was Ianthe! A lifeless corpse! No color was upon her cheek, nor her lip; but about her face a stillness almost as attaching as in the life that once dwelt there; upon her neck and breast was blood, and upon her throat were the marks of teeth having opened the veins. Victims? Egos demanding sustenance.

And, if you think the Power of my feeding does not destroy, remember them, and their families.

Fanny Imlay

Harriet Shelley

Clara Shelley

William Shelley

Or the creation and destruction of Poe...

And the damnation of Stoker, dead from the very substance from which flowed his literary genius...blood, always blood.

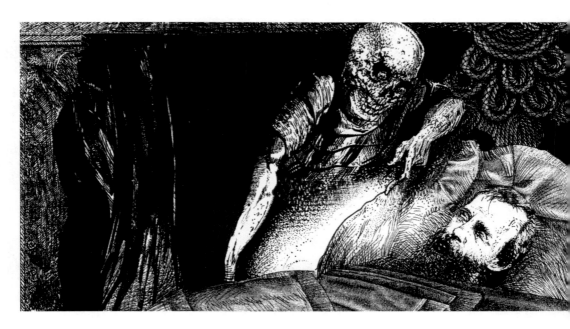

Look back, then, and recognise me—the Greatest Storyteller of Horror!

And now, now, with the fields of Europe soaked in the blood of millions, I will move on. There are two delectable leads. First, a new phenomenon in the Caribbean—a new form of Un-Dead—not my old friends the vampyres, but shambling men and women they call *zombi*. Soon I sail for Haiti to seek the *zombis*, and a soul to spread the tale to your disbelieving rational world.

The other? As my instincts took me to 16th Century England they now tell me to visit a budding writer in *New* England. So far he has yet to deliver much more than poetry and a story published just this month, with a title that recalls my time with the Philistines—*Dagon*. These centuries I've searched for another who would benefit from my attentions and this man feels dark, very dark. His name resonates. Lovecraft, shall we play?

Goodbye, friends, for now. Think of me as you succumb to the pleasures of horror, and anticipate the day when *you'll* become the story's central character.

Afterword

In our tale Victor Frankenstein met with his Monster in an Ice-Cave on Montanvert near Chamonix in the French Alps, there to debate the ethics and responsibilities of creation, much as he did in Mary Shelley's classic novel. One might think only three creatures ever knew *exactly* what was said that fateful day—the two antagonists and Shelley, the author of *Frankenstein, or The Modern Prometheus*. But, as in all great fiction, what appears on the surface is less than the full story. A fourth observer was later able to report on events—and now you know his visage, if not his name.

When it came to tell *his* story I was confronted with choices as to exactly what dialog and narrative might best serve. Appeasing the Greatest Storyteller of Horror is no easy task—the ancient collector of tales fabulous and true is an uneasy collaborator and an unrelenting taskmaster.

It had been years since I read the great classics that make up this long graphic tale. In the joy of discovery was born a commitment to ensure this particular retelling would be true to the originals.

In one notable case it was clear the original dialog and narrative best present the tale. Wherever possible in *Frankenstein* I used Mary Shelley's words. This was not always entirely viable, so sometimes I had to write Victorian English narration or dialog. There were also times I had to adjust Mary's text to suit the graphic novel form, but I hope I did so with care for both her legacy and my readers. However, the conversations between those who were at the Villa Diodati that fateful night are cut wholly from my imagination (or perhaps channeled via our Old Friend).

This book often deals with real lives (or imagined, in the case of Shakespeare, whose mid-years are unknown to history) and there I tried not only to deliver a solidly grounded imagination of their tragedies but also, if possible, to use their real words. For instance, the opening lines of this graphic novel are Lord Byron's:

> From peak to peak, the rattling crags among
> Leaps the live thunder! Not from one lone cloud,
> But every mountain now hath found a tongue,
> And Jura answers, through her misty shroud,
> Back to the joyous Alps, who call to her aloud!

While *Frankenstein* is best served with words as close to those in the actual novel as possible, this was not the case with Polidori's prose in *The Vampyre* section, excepting a few quotes from the actual characters. Frankly, the good doctor's prose is too turgid for my taste, or yours.

Afterword

I used the real words of those who suffered "the Curse of the Diodati," such as Harriet Shelley's suicide note.

Moving on to Shakespeare, readers will of course recognize:

> *Double, double*
> *toile and trouble;*
> *Fire burne, and*
> *Caldron bubble.*

And his *All the world's a stage* line takes on new import considering what has now revealed by the Storyteller. On the shores of the New World it was pure joy to quote Poe, even for just a few delectable words of each tale.

This book's last adaptation is of Stoker's *Dracula* and here, again, a few words—mostly the Count's, or those of Van Helsing, are direct quotes. The epistolary form of the novel and Stoker's style meant this was more difficult to achieve than it had been with Shelley. In so many ways, *Dracula* is a much more "modern" novel than *Frankenstein* and flows more like a modern cinematic adventure, allowing an interpretive narrative, enhanced by Glenn Chadbourne's mindbending illustrations.

Finally, I can confirm the words of the Storyteller are *entirely* his own.

Rocky Wood